SO MY CHILDREN WILL KNOW

A book about Jesus…
        for anyone who doesn't know

Joyce Wiles

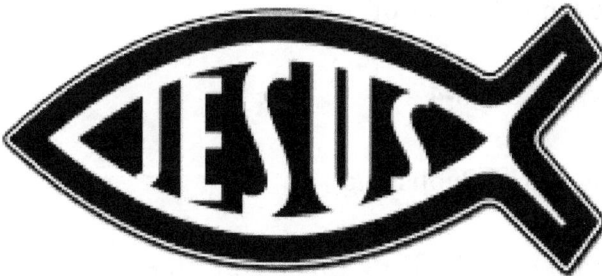

SO MY CHILDREN WILL KNOW
A book about Jesus...
for anyone who doesn't know

Copyright © 2021 Joyce P. Wiles

FIRST EDITION

Cover Design: Joyce P. Wiles

Printed in the United States of America

ISBN 978-0-578-75808-4

Distributed by Adriel Publishing

Life Application Bible by Holy Bible. New International Version (NIV). Copyright © 1991 Tyndale House Publishers, Wheaton, IL, & Zondervan Publishing House, Grand Rapids, MI.

This book is dedicated to all my children and grandchildren. It explains my love for Jesus, because He has always loved me... even before I knew Him. It encompasses all the things about Jesus that I have always wanted to share with my family so they could never say, "I just didn't know".

What people are saying about this book...

"My husband and I have been friends with Joyce Wiles, both personally and professionally, for over 25 years. Joyce lives out her faith with the wonderful combination of "showing mercy" and "speaking truth" and these loving traits are reflected on every page in her book, So My Children Will Know. I highly recommend Joyce's book, because not only does she share her own personal story and relationship with Christ, but you can hear her heart (and the Lord's heart) for family and friends coming through loud and clear on each page. If you have loved ones you've been trying to reach for Christ, you will be inspired, empowered and encouraged by this book!"

Beth Jones
Pastor & Author

"Joyce Wiles' book will inspire you with her story of how God took her from a difficult childhood to great success in the real estate business through an abiding faith in the Word of God. The scriptures that supported her will encourage, comfort, and serve as a firm foundation on which to strengthen your own faith in Jesus. I highly recommend you send it to your children or grandchildren."

Mary Jane Mapes
International Speaker & Author

TABLE OF CONTENTS

INTRODUCTION:

This writing is from my heart. It is for my children so they will know and understand God's love for them, His Perfect Plan for their lives, and for anyone else who doesn't know Jesus:

>*Ephesians 3:18 Paul's Prayer:*
>*"And may you have the power to*
>*understand; as all God's people*
>*should, how wide, how long, how*
>*high, and how deep his love is."*

How do I keep it simple? Because it is so simple. It's as simple as black and white. How do I keep it simple enough that you become so hungry, so eager to grasp this total joy and happiness that awaits you...now, this very day!

I have walked this journey and wasted 30+ years of my life trying to do it **"my way,"** trying to work hard enough to have what I needed, trying to fix family issues, marriages, and everything else in between, trying to be good enough so God would accept me.

For that reason, I have inserted the various phases of my personal walk (MY STORY – NOTES). I never realized it didn't have to be this way.

Over the years I have made notations of various scriptures and readings. Things I wanted to share with my own children; but there is never the right time. One blessing from our pandemic is that I've had the opportunity to put these thoughts and scriptures into a book for all ages, adult, grandchildren, nieces, nephews, etc.

Maybe they have known Jesus from their childhood days, but as adults have walked away. So many families today just don't seem to have the time. And some just think when they are ready, then, they will consider looking into it. Sadly, others have been influenced by our media and education system that "God is dead."

His birth, death and resurrection were all prophesied in the Old Testament **700+ years before He was born.** (Over 400 prophesies). Genesis, Deuteronomy, Jeremiah, Micah and Zechariah all prophesy the Saviors birth, life, death and resurrection. That He would be born in Bethlehem, from the lineage of King David, there would be a massacre of children in His birthplace. He would bear the sins of many. He would be denied, spit upon, not rebuke his accusers, led to slaughter like a lamb, not decay in a grave, etc.

Can you even believe that?! **700 years before His birth.**

His Word:

> *"Behold," he wrote, "a virgin shall conceive, and bear a son, and shall call his name Immanuel."*
> *(Isaiah 7:14)*

"And the spirit of the Lord shall rest upon him, the spirit of wisdom and understanding, the spirit of counsel and might, the spirit of knowledge and of the fear of the Lord." (Isaiah 53:3)

Isaiah wrote that the Savior wouldn't judge people by what He could see on the outside or by what He heard, but He would judge people with righteousness, knowing what was in their hearts. (Isaiah 11:2-4)

His Word:

"He was despised and rejected by mankind, a man of suffering, and familiar with pain. Like one from whom people hide their faces, he was despised, and we held him in low esteem. "He was wounded for our transgressions, he was bruised for our iniquities [wrongdoings]; and with his stripes we are healed." (Isaiah 53:4-5)

"But you, O Bethlehem Ephratah, are only a small village among all the people of Judah. Yet a ruler of Israel will come from you, one whose origins are from the distant past ... And he will stand to lead his flock with the LORD's strength, in the majesty of the name of the LORD his God. Then his people will live there undisturbed, for he will be highly honored around the world. And he will be the source of peace."
(Micah 5:2–5)

"But he was pierced for our transgressions, he was crushed for our iniquities; the punishment that brought us peace was on him, and by his wounds we are healed. We all, like sheep, have gone astray, each of us has turned to our own way; and the LORD has laid on him the iniquity of us all. He was oppressed and afflicted, yet he did not open his mouth; he was led like a lamb to the slaughter, and as a sheep before its shearers is silent, so he did

not open his mouth. By oppression[a] and judgment he was taken away. Yet who of his generation protested? For he was cut off from the land of the living; for the transgression of my people he was punished.[b] He was assigned a grave with the wicked, and with the rich in his death, though he had done no violence, nor was any deceit in his mouth. Yet it was the LORD's will to crush him and cause him to suffer, and though the LORD makes[c] his life an offering for sin, he will see his offspring and prolong his days, and the will of the LORD will prosper in his hand. After he has suffered, he will see the light of life[d] and be satisfied[e]; by his knowledge[f] my righteous servant will justify many, and he will bear their iniquities. Therefore I will give him a portion among the great,[g] and he will divide the spoils with the strong,[h] because he poured out his life unto death, and was numbered with the transgressors. For he bore the sin of many, and made intercession for the transgressors." (Isaiah 53:5-12)

Jesus would "preach good tidings unto the meek" and would "bind up the brokenhearted," and "proclaim liberty to the captives." (Isaiah 61:1)

"Rejoice greatly, Daughter Zion! Shout, Daughter Jerusalem! See, your your king comes to you, righteous and victorious, lowly and riding on a donkey, on a colt, the foal of a donkey." (Zechariah 9:9)

"And I will pour out on the house of David and the inhabitants of Jerusalem a spirit of grace and supplication. They will look on me, the one they have pierced, and they will mourn for him as one mourns for an only child and grieve bitterly for him as one grieves for a firstborn son." (Zechariah 12:10)

"Because you will not abandon me
to the realm of the dead, nor will you
let your faithful[a] one see decay."
(Psalms 16:10)

"But God will redeem me from the
realm of the dead; he will surely
take me to himself." (Psalms 49:15)

Jesus was the pure, unblemished "lamb" who had to be sacrificed so that we could be forgiven of our sinful life and live with God in Heaven when we **choose** to believe.

Life doesn't wait for **"your time."** Life happens every day. Make it the **"best"** life now. There may not be a tomorrow. Please don't waste another day, another hour, trying to do it all by yourself, seeking help and support from friend, family or anyone who will listen and still not getting the answers! God is listening...Jesus is calling your name. He can make a way, when there is no way. He is the same yesterday, today and tomorrow.

CHAPTER 1

WHAT IF?

What if...you knew every day for the rest of your life, regardless of any circumstances, you could have peace in your heart, laying your head on your pillow at night in complete rest? Would you want that peace?

What if...you saw an advertisement for a new product that could heal and remove ALL pain and disease in your life? Would you want to immediately run out and purchase that product?

What if....someone came along in your life and blessed you abundantly, more than you could ever imagine, enough to eliminate all your worries and concerns? Would that person become your new best friend!

What if...you knew for certain, that when you die and leave this earth, you would see the face of God with Jesus at His right hand and know that all your sins had been forgiven AND forgotten; that you would live in Heaven with your loved ones who have gone before you, and behold their beautiful faces again? Would you seize that comfort?

AND,......What if...you were given an invisible mentor, advisor, or counselor; someone who could impart to you untold wisdom and guidance in every aspect of your life. He would live with you every minute of every day to help you make the perfect decisions for your life, your family, your work? Would your door be open?

What if...there was always something/ someone you could reach out to, hold on to, to get you through the down times, the struggles, the depression and be able to ascribe to a positive, uplifting, overcomer attitude? Would you take hold and never let go?

The answer to ALL these questions is a simple one: **Jesus Christ**

You say, *"do I have to be perfect to receive these things? Surely, there must be something I must do to receive His love, His promises, His gifts, this special peace, His guidance? I can't be perfect; I make mistakes every day. I say the wrong things sometime. I get angry. My employer doesn't treat me right, my husband doesn't help out, the kids drive me crazy...and I like to have a drink with my buddies occasionally...and...I just can't be perfect! I'll wait until I can get better control over my life, I'll wait until I'm good enough for God to accept me and then I'll do all these wonderful things."*

Well, you might be surprised to know that … No, you don't have to do anything except "BELIEVE".

Jesus died on the cross for ALL our transgressions. He was tortured and crucified for all our sins. No one can ever be "good enough", no one could ever think to be perfect, except one, Jesus Christ. Just BELIEVE in Him, BELIEVE His Word, the Bible, His total Instruction Book.

Many people think **"if"** I accept Jesus, I'll have to lose my friends, stop going to the bars, not have any fun, etc. You really don't! When you begin to rely on the Holy Spirit, your life supernaturally changes. It's not something you do intentionally, but the more you read God's Word, the more your choices start to change, new friends appear, your desire for unhealthy things begins to dwindle, your heart opens, you see things differently, you want to spend more time with Him.

His Word:

> *"This righteousness is given through faith in Jesus Christ to all who believe. There is for all have sinned and fall short of the glory of God."*
> *(Romans 3:22-23)*

Many witnessed the love of Christ. They witnessed His miracles. They heard the parables and the words He spoke as a messenger from God, His Son, teaching them of God's love and mercy, His grace and how we could have eternal life. They followed Him by the thousands!

His Word:

> *"Then Jesus told him, "Because you have seen me, you have believed;   blessed are those who have not seen me and yet have believed." (John 20:29)*

You cannot buy His love. You could never do enough good deeds to earn his love. It is totally free! We are not, cannot be justified by our good works or deeds so that no one can boast of his accomplishments for God's favor. We are only justified by our faith, by BELIEVING!

It doesn't get any simpler than that!

MY STORY – Note 1:

My own life would be called dysfunctional, being raised in a strict Italian household with three younger siblings, a father with mental issues and a mother whose love held us together. I was the only daughter of a man whose only sister had become pregnant at 16. That was not going to happen to his family. I know he loved us in his own way, but his uncontrollable anger kept us in fear, never knowing what to expect. He would control by mentally and verbally abusing us, (sometimes physically) with his unpredictability and his own insecurities. As I approached my teens, and my mother began working outside the home, my life became extremely more troubling. I attempted suicide at 17.

Through our mother's love and guidance, my brothers and I learned there was a God. On Sundays our father would drive us to the nearest church, drop us off, then pick us up, never bothering to attend. Since Sunday mornings were the only private time my parents might have, our mother wasn't allowed to go to church with us. For my first nine years of school, we moved every year to a new rental home so the nearest church might be Baptist, Catholic, Presbyterian or whatever. There was no structure, no support, only the love of our mother who taught us that Jesus loved us, died on the cross for us and that we would go to Heaven when we died. That was what we did know.

"Christianity revolves around one central Person: Jesus Christ. Jesus is the most unique Person in history. He claimed to be God! This claim puts Jesus in a different league than any other religious leader in history."

Beth Jones
Author
Getting A Grip On The Basics

CHAPTER 2

GOD'S WORD -- THE BIBLE

From the days of Moses, prophets were God's way of communicating. The Jews are God's chosen people. As a Jewish infant Moses had been spared by his mother hiding him in the bullrushes from the evil Egyptians. The Egyptians were pagans who had heard rumors that a new king, a Jew, had been born, one who would rule the world. They set out to murder all young children under the age of two.

As it happened, Moses was discovered by an Egyptian princess who raised him as her own. He was not perfect. He had a speech impediment. He was not a public speaker. As an adult it was discovered that he was a Jew, therefore, deemed a slave. As such, he watched as God's people, his people, were beaten and tortured mercilessly. This was the man God chose to lead His people, the Jews, to freedom, out of Egypt to the land God had promised them. The journey is called **"The Exodus,"** the second book of the Bible.

Moses led them as God directed. How could any mere human bring about the ten plagues over Egypt which resulted in Pharaoh finally allowing the Jewish people to leave? Pharaoh was warned by Moses of each plague before it ever occurred, i.e., the rivers turning to blood, frogs covering the whole land, lice and gnats, flies, death of livestock, boils covering their bodies, hail destroying crops, locust infestation, total darkness. Pharaoh remained hard hearted until the death of his infant son. As the Jews began their exodus, Pharaoh would not refrain, sending his army after them. By the hand of God, the seas were split wide open letting the people pass through before closing in on Pharaoh's army. How did all this happen? With just a mere man? There were witnesses to all the events...they were recorded...How does this happen?

Overcoming many rebellions of his own people and discouragement along the way, Moses relied on God's divine guidance to continue the exodus. God appeared to Moses in a dark cloud, directing him to come forth to the top of the mountain. Forty days later he returned to his assembly who had also witnessed the voice of God:

His Word:

> *"Then Moses led the people out of the camp to meet with God, and they stood at the foot of the mountain. Mount Sinai was covered with smoke, because the Lord descended on it in fire. The smoke billowed up from it like smoke from a furnace, and the whole mountain trembled violently. As the sound of the trumpet grew louder and louder, Moses spoke and and the voice of God answered him. (Exodus 19:17-19)*

After Moses, there were other prophets who were directed by God. The fulfillment of their prophecies proving they were divine and from God (not just any man). There were also many false prophets whose prophesies could only bring results through trickery and sorcery, who were soon found out. They could not compete with God's chosen few. The prophets of God are the authors of the Old Testament, men who received His word, shared His word, lived His word.

Most important was the prophet Isaiah in the Old Testament.

Approximately 700+/- years before the birth of Christ, the prophet Isaiah revealed that a Savior would be born of a Virgin, that He would be called Immanuel, who would be from the line of David, would heal the sick and blind, raise the dead. He would be spat upon and widely rejected, sought by the Gentiles, would be our substitute, would bear our sins and sorrows, would voluntarily accept our guilt and punishment for sin, bearing the sins of many for the sake of their salvation as a blood atonement. He would be disfigured by suffering, God's spirit would be upon Him, and He would be exalted. He would be buried in a rich man's grave and resurrected on the third day: our Savior Jesus Christ.

All predicted **700+ years before his birth.** Do you get that? Just as it was written...How does this just happen? How did Isaiah know all the details? Can you even predict what tomorrow will bring?

If we can believe the authenticity of the prophets, the prophecy of Isaiah, how can we not believe in Jesus Christ? If we can believe in Jesus Christ, why would we dare to deny His Father's word, the Bible? If we believe His Word, why would we not follow his direction, his instruction, his guidance...all the way to a life of peace and fulfillment.

His Word:

> *"And suddenly a voice came*
> *from heaven, saying, 'This is my*
> *beloved son, whom I love, with him*
> *I am well pleased.'" (Matthew 3:17)*

"He has delivered us from the domain of darkness and transferred us to the kingdom of his beloved son." (Colossians 1:13)

"Look at my servant, whom I have chosen. He is my beloved who pleases me. I will put my Spirit upon him, and he will proclaim justice to the nations." (Matthew 12:18)

Chapter 3

Perfect Peace

What if you knew every day for the rest of your life, regardless of any circumstances, you could have peace in your heart, resting your head on your pillow at night in complete rest? Would you want that peace?

In this world, we are surrounded by worry, fear, anxiety, unknowns we can't control. Financial concerns overtake our dreams at night. Relationships, health and emotional well-being of our family members and loved ones invade our lives daily. Work is so demanding, so many decisions to make. So many things to do, so many responsibilities, so many worries!

His Word:

> *"Do not be anxious about anything,*
> *but in every situation, by prayer*
> *and petition, with thanksgiving,*
> *present your requests to God. And*
> *the peace of God, which transcends*
> *all understanding, will guard your*
> *hearts and your minds in Christ*
> *Jesus." (Philippians 4:6-7)*

This means a peace that is unbelievable to our own human understanding. How is it that when life is falling apart around us and all hope is gone, we can yet turn to God, holding on to Him, and receive His comfort and peace. There is no other peace except through Him. There is no peace without Him.

His Word:

> *"For I know the thoughts that I have*
> *for you", declares the Lord, "plans*
> *to prosper you and not to harm you,*
> *to give you hope and a future."*
> *(Jeremiah 29:11)*

"I have told you these things, so that in me you may have peace. In this world you will have trouble. But take heart! I have overcome the world."
(John 16:33)

"Peace I leave with you. My peace I give to you, not as the world gives do I give to you. Let not your heart be troubled, neither let it be afraid."
(John 14:27)

"And His name shall be called Wonderful, Counselor, Mighty God, Everlasting Father, Prince of Peace."
(Isaiah 9:6)

"to shine on those living in darkness and in the shadow of death, to guide our feet into the path of peace."
(Luke 1:79)

David in *Psalms 30:11 says, "You turned my wailing into dancing; you removed my sackcloth and*

clothed me with joy, that my heart
may sing your praises and not be
silent. Lord, my God, I will praise
you forever."

You may know the story of David, the smallest in his family who worked the flocks, a shepherd boy who daily worshiped the Lord as he watched over the sheep. So unassuming, happy with his lot in life, his music, his songs. God chose him to take down Goliath (a Philistine giant over 9 feet tall), the lowliest to overcome the fiercest! David eventually became King of Israel. God knew that David was a man after God's own heart.

God loved him dearly...but David was a human. He made many mistakes, sinned, became egotistical, was an adulterer, and even a murderer. The Psalms are full of David's love of God, his mistakes, of his lamentations when he failed, his confessions when he sinned...But, more importantly was his love for God, his BELIEF in God, always praising God, and asking for forgiveness. He was human but he never forgot his God who forgives, who gave him supernatural strength, who led his path to kingdom. God never forgot David!

This world can entice us into many situations. We want to be independent. We think that we can handle everything. "We" are in control… but, how many nights have you lain awake trying to sort out problems, finances, marriage issues, temptations you are fighting? Is there anyone who has not? Who can you call in the middle of the night?

Knowing God means knowing that no matter the time of day or night, you can talk to Him. He's always listening. He likes to hear your voice. He desires a relationship with you. He is your heavenly Father. Can you even imagine that someone can love you to that extent and more than you love your own children? God loves you more!

His Word:

"Come to Me, all you who are weary and burdened, and I will give you rest. Take my yoke upon you and learn from Me, for I am gentle and humble in heart and you will find rest for your souls. For My yoke is easy and My burden is light. (Matthew 11: 28-30)

MY STORY - Note 2

I hesitate to even share this childish experience that has brought me immeasurable peace for many years now. In difficult times, as I lay in bed with all my worries swirling in my head, finances, relationships, family crisis, etc. and sleep was far away, I began thinking about Jesus and His love for me. I began singing in my head, "Jesus Loves Me...this I know for the bible tells me so...little ones to Him belong, they are weak but He is strong. Yes, Jesus loves me, Yes, Jesus loves me." Often when our worries are so BIG, we can feel like little, helpless children. Do you know that even now, as soon as my head hits the pillow, that song comes to mind. When those words are in your head, (or any praise song) satan's darts can never prevail.

His Word:

> **"He listens to the godly person who does His will." (John 9:31)**

> **"For the eyes of the Lord are on the righteous and His ears are attentive to their prayer; but the face of the Lord is against those who do evil." (1 Peter: 3:12)**

> **"And if we know that He hears us – whatever we ask – we know that we have what we asked of him." (1 John 5:15)**

MY STORY – Note 3

As an adult, needless to say, old childhood patterns remained. Looking for peace at 18, I ran away and married a young man I had only known for 3 months. Peace did not come. The marriage lasted 7 years and produced one beautiful daughter. Next step, divorce. Now…I had the freedom to get out into the world and do "my own thing".

At 27, I married again, to someone 12 years older and well educated. Within a short period we had two more beautiful daughters, and had begun two businesses. I learned much during those years and I began to develop self-confidence. After twelve years, my husband's alcohol abuse led to divorce. Many more mistakes would be made over the next 17 years. Still no peace. I did go to church on Sundays, taking my now "three" children. Still knowing I was forgiven and would go to Heaven… but where was my peace? I needed help now!

I certainly was not perfect by any means but I did pray, asking for peace, for finances, for help. Always "asking," "asking," wondering "where is God?"…never thinking to thank Him for the little things, never thinking to be grateful for what I already had…Then…it happened! Another disaster! After only four months working in a new company, new state, new home, and a new career, the company collapsed and filed bankruptcy. I was in a strange place, unemployed, divorced, with three children to take care of, no one to turn to...I was preparing once again to relocate to another city, another state, start all over, move my children to another school, try to be closer my family. Still being hopeful and taking my children to church, still "asking," still "praying".

A few weeks into my drama, one Sunday after returning from church, and just after searching the classifieds, I received a call from a local banker with an amazing opportunity. An opportunity that would seal my future with numerous successes and I would not have to move! A phone call on a Sunday afternoon? The best opportunity of my lifetime? Someone knew someone who knew I had worked on the now failed project. The banker calling me on a Sunday afternoon to introduce me to the new owner. How does that just happen? God's Plan!

As I thought about my circumstances, I stood at my bedroom window, so thankful. I opened my Bible, asking, 'God, why are you so good to *me?????' I am so far from perfect, I sin, I make so many mistakes. As I opened a new modern version Bible I had picked up in a motel room, looking for a reading that would give me answers, a page opened to Romans 3:22. God's Plan!*

His Word:

> **"For all have sinned and fallen
> short of the glory of God". No one
> is "good" enough for Salvation.
> Only by ACCEPTING and
> BELIEVING are we redeemed so
> that no man can boast that he is
> better than another." (Romans 3:22)**

No one had ever told me. I just didn't know His acceptance was free! I thought I had to buy my way into God's graces by being good enough! Never sinning! I kept failing! I was wrong! Everyone sins. No one person could ever be as perfect as Jesus, no matter how hard we try. He loves us. He forgives us.

I was so thankful, so grateful for his acceptance and love of me even though I wasn't perfect. I fell on my knees and asked God to forgive me and to be my Lord and Savior for the rest of my life. That was the beginning of my true relationship with God... and He has never failed me. That doesn't mean that **"I"** didn't make any more bad choices. I did and lived the results. BUT, it did mean that He would always walk me through them to the other side, to the place He wanted me to be, a better place than I could ever imagine. He is my Rock and my Shield!

His Word:

> *"Keep your lives free from the worry of money; and be content with what you have, because God has said, 'Never will I leave you, never will I forsake you."*
> *(Hebrews 13:5)*

> *"In the good times he walks right beside us and in the bad he carries*

us. We are never left alone in this world. We may be in it but we are definitely not of it." (John 15:19)

As the song goes, He becomes your, *"Way Maker, Miracle Worker, Promise Keeper, Light In The Darkness, My God, that is who you are".*

MY STORY – Note 4

Looking back through my journey in life with various struggles, marriages, relationships, disappointments, I can see dramatically God's hand on my life from the moment I believed. My bad choices in relationships had created many tears, heartaches and loneliness. Many Sundays after my children were grown, I would find myself sitting in church alone. I would notice married couples sitting next to each other, the husband's arm around his wife's shoulder. I would think to myself, "I know that couple could get through anything. They have God's blessing on their life. They are serving and worshiping Him together."

Little did I see God's plan coming together in my own life!

Beginning a new career in real estate development, I picked up a simple floor call meant for someone else in our office. Someone who happened to be away for the next few weeks. (How do these things "just" happen?) His Plan!

The clients happened to be young pastors with four small children and a church membership of around 100, meeting in a small house. They were looking for something a little larger. I was told by my office peers, "Don't work with those churches. They never have money and they will run you all over and never buy anything!" The couple reminded me of my brother and his family back in North Carolina. They became my church family. Not only was I blessed financially over and over, but I was blessed to watch and help them grow and expand over the next 25 years to a church of 128,000 square feet, attendance approaching 3,000 members.

Their love of God and His Word enriched my relationship with Jesus Christ. I was fed with classes and teachings like I had never experienced in any church. Relationships developed with friends that became family and I was truly blessed.

It was during this time that I met my husband of 20+ years. He was new to the church and eager for all the classes and teachings I had just experienced. Now, we sit in church on Sundays and hold hands. As in all things of this world, there have been occasional roadblocks. Satan is always lurking in the background waiting for an opportunity to steal, kill or destroy the goodness of God. But... "we can do all things through Christ who gives us strength". He walks us through every time. Christ is an overcomer, therefore, if we have the Spirit of Christ, we, too, are over comers!

God has blessed us in so many ways in our marriage, with our blended family, in our work, in our play. We see His hand in everything we do and we are blessed to have found each other. (in God's dwelling place). We have His Perfect Peace!

I want to share the exact words of a pastoral friend who last year lost his beautiful 7-year- old daughter. In this most difficult time his faith has brought him peace.

"Today we celebrate my daughter's Birthday, not on earth, but in Heaven! When I think about what is happening in society in 2020, I want to challenge you to "Stay In Faith - Never Put Down Your Faith!" I do know why I am able to celebrate today even when I have an unimaginable pain - I do know why I'm not breaking down in grief - I do know how I'm able to fight in faith against the kingdom of darkness every minute of the day that has an assignment to destroy my purpose - I do know why I'm ready to minister and lead people into their promised land - I do know why my dad told me yesterday that I have been a voice during this crisis - I do know why my stepdad and my former coach told me today that I'm a great man! I know that I can, and will continue to be an Agent of Change for the rest of my days until I see my princess again because FAITH SAVED ME! Please understand that my Faith Saved Me! In these times of pain, tension and unrest things may be overwhelming sometimes, but if I can overcome so can you! What I feel in my body, emotions and mind I can't describe, but like my Pastor told me yesterday, "you are winning!" We are people that

you know have faced the greatest tragedy that a family can face but refuse to let down our faith. So, that means you can stand too! No matter what you face, all you have to do is "Have Faith in God! Never think for one moment that real faith doesn't change the natural because it has changed everything in our lives! When you have to fight for your peace every moment of the day, I love Jesus so much that He taught me Faith! So, whatever has come to discourage you...when you overcome it, and you will..."He will say, your FAITH HAS SAVED YOU!!!" Luke 7:50

This servant has **FAITH**. He has **PEACE**. Thank you, Jesus!

Chapter 4

Blessings -- Part 1

What if someone came along in your life and blessed you abundantly, more than you could ever imagine, enough to cover all your debt plus your dreams?

Would that person become your new BFF?

Abundance does not always mean "money". It can mean money...but we can also be blessed by abundant peace, abundant health, abundant friends, abundance of love, abundance of contentment with our lot in life, etc. They are all blessings!

But, is there anyone out there who has "never" worried over finances? We have to support our families. Life happens, we lose our jobs, unforeseen health issues arise, transportation problems, etc. Finances are high up on the list of reasons marriages fail, families fall apart, depression settles in.

His Word:

> *"Therefore, I tell you, whatever you ask for in prayer, believe that you have received it, and it will be yours." (Mark 11:24)*

When we realize and accept that **"everything"** we have is a gift from God, i.e., your spouse was put into your path from the beginning, your children are a gift from God, the opportunity of finding your workplace, your ability or health to be able to work and bring home a paycheck. All these things came from God. He is our source.

He makes ALL things possible, not you.

For some, this is a hard pill to swallow. Many live by the **"I Did It My Way"** philosophy.

"Look at me, look at what I've made of myself, look at what I've accomplished."
Sorry to say! God is working His plan!

God knew you before you were born.

He has always been there, making opportunities, opening doors, providing. Remember? He is your Father. He loves you just like you love your own children. You want the best for them, and you'll do anything you can to help them, to lead them. Christ wants the best for you, His children. He will do everything He can for you if you will only **BELIEVE.**

His Word:

> *"The thief comes to steal, kill and destroy; I have come that they might have life, and that they have it abundantly!! (John 10:10)*
> *"You let people ride over our heads, we went through fire and water; but...you brought us to a place of abundance." (Psalms 66:12)*

> *"The grace of our Lord was poured*
> *out on me abundantly, along with the*
> *faith and love that are in Christ Jesus."*
> *(1 Timothy 1:14)*

> *"And God is able to bless you*
> *abundantly so that in all things at*
> *all times having all that you need,*
> *you will abound in every good work."*
> *(2 Corinthians 9:8)*

He is willing and able, anxious, to give you the desires of your heart.

His Word:

> *"Take delight in the Lord, and*
> *He will give you the desires of*
> *your heart." (Psalms 37:4)*

The hardest part is acknowledging that there is someone greater than "you". That you were never in control. God has blessed you with opportunity and good health to accomplish all you have. He is waiting for your acceptance, waiting for you to recognize his Love for you, waiting for your acknowledgement and waiting for your praise. It can be extremely difficult letting go, realizing that you must humble yourself, do away with pride and submit to a Higher Power who has had your back through everything in your life.

His Word:

> *"Thus, saith the Lord, Let not the wise (man) glory in his wisdom, neither let the mighty (man) glory in his might, let not the rich (man) glory in his riches." (Jeremiah 9:23)*

> *"Do you see a person wise in his own eyes? There is more hope for a fool than for them." (Proverbs 26:12)*

> *"Humble yourself before the Lord, and He will lift you up." (James 4:10)*

> *"Pride goes before destruction, a haughty spirit before a fall." (Proverbs 16:18)*

"But when his heart became arrogant and hardened with pride, he was deposed from his royal throne and stripped of his glory."
(Daniel 5:20)

Everyone wants to feel important and self sufficient. But when we sit back and let God do the driving...his gifts surpass anything we could ever imagine! You've probably heard the **"let go and let God"** phrase. Surrender to the fullest so that He can prove His Word, His love.

His Word:

"Come unto me all who labor and are heavy laden and I will give you rest. You used to live in sin, just like the rest of the world, obeying the devil – the commander of the powers in the unseen world. He is the spirit at work in the hearts of those who refuse to obey God."
(Ephesians 2:2)

MY STORY – Note 5

We have freedoms and opportunities in this country where God has placed us. That in itself is an amazing blessing we should always remember! He placed us here! I had always heard, "In America, you can do anything you chose to do!"

So...the first 30 years of my adult life I tried to do things "my way", struggling, taking on heavy burdens, working 3 jobs to support my children, not letting go! Why didn't I just give my burden to God? I just didn't know...I had labored and struggled. Why hadn't someone explained to me? It's not about "me"! It's about Him!

His Word:

"Come to me all you who are weary and burdened, and I will give you rest." (Matthew 11:28)

He gives us guidance, wisdom. Once I knew Him, many of the things "I" thought I had to have, I thought were important, that I "needed", weren't important after all. He showed me His ways of how to do things and opened doors I had never considered.

His Word:

"Therefore, everyone who hears these words of mine and puts them into practice is like a wise man who built his house on the rock." (Matthew 7:24)

"For to the man who pleases Him, God gives wisdom, knowledge and joy." (Ecclesiastes 2:26)

"Also, that every man eat and drink,`and enjoy good in all his labor, is the gift of God." (Ecclesiastes 3:13)

"Therefore, I tell you, do not be anxious for your life, what you will eat, what you will drink; nor yet for your body, what you will wear." (Matthew 6:25)

"But seek first God's Kingdom, and his righteousness, and all these things will be given to you as well." (Matthew 6:33)

"Do not merely listen to the Word, and so deceive yourselves. Do what it says." (James 1:22)

"The Lord doesn't always remove the sources of stress in our lives...but He's always there and cares for us. We can feel His arms around us on the darkest night."

Dr. James C. Dobson
Founder Focus on the Family
Author & Psychologist

CHAPTER 5

BLESSINGS -- PART 2

So...you've accepted Christ, you know when you die you will go to Heaven. But...where are all the benefits? The gifts? The abundance? The blessings?

"Wait for it..." Whenever you visit a church, you're always waiting for that embarrassing moment when they ask for money! You are thinking to yourself, ***"they have a huge facility, they have plenty. Look at what they drive, they dress like a million bucks. They can't need 'my' money! My family needs it more than the church, look at all these people? Maybe later when I get that raise or when my ship comes in."***

If we agree and accept God as our Savior, our Provider, our Source, how can we deliberately ignore His Word regarding our finances. He has provided us with everything. We have nothing without Him!

God gives you the motivation, opens doors for your employment, hands you the opportunity, health to do a good job, favor in the workplace.

And, you say **"Look what I did."** His was the greatest sacrifice of mankind. God's bride is the church. We support the church because it supports His glory. Regardless of what you may **"think"** the church uses the money for... That is between your church and God.

God knows the hearts of His servants. He knows how they honor Him in their disbursements, just as He knows your heart in giving it! Christ loved the Church. We honor our Creator when we tithe!

His Word:

"Husbands, love your wives, as Christ loved the church and gave Himself up for her."
(Ephesians 5:25)

"And I tell you, you are Peter, and on this rock I will build my church and the gates of hell shall not prevail against it."
(Matthew 16:18)

"Pay careful attention to yourselves and to all the flock, in which the Holy Spirit has made you overseers, to care for the church of God, which He obtained with his own blood."
(Acts 20:28)

"Let the elders who rule, well be considered worthy of double honor, especially those who labor in preaching and teaching."
(I Timothy 5:17)

"It is more blessed to give than to receive." (Acts 20:25)

"Jesus sat down opposite the place where the offerings were put and watched the crowd putting their money into the temple treasury. Many rich people threw in large amounts. But a poor widow came and put in two very small copper coins, worth only a fraction of a penny. Calling his disciples to him, Jesus said, "I tell you the truth, this poor widow has put more into the treasury than all the others. They all gave out of their wealth; but she, out of her poverty, put in everything—all she had to live on." (Mark 12:41-44)

We are saved and guaranteed Heaven when we accept Christ, confess our sins and ask forgiveness. But His Word promises so much more. We don't have to wait until we get to Heaven to enjoy God's gifts. Hearing, believing and following his instructions will open up the storehouses surrounding our everyday lives. He expects us to be good stewards of all that He provides.

The good steward upon receiving his weekly, monthly salary, already has a budget scheduled to cover housing, food, auto, insurance, medical, college fund for the children, etc. Is your tithe in that budget? Would you rob God? He has given it all to you. Do you trust Him enough to give back 10%? Do you **"believe"** enough to watch your storehouses overflow. Many today live through His promises. The Lord says, "**test**" me in this. What do you have to lose when there is so much to gain?

His Word:

> *"Will a man rob God? Yet you rob me. But you ask, 'How do we rob you?' In tithes and offerings."*
> *(Malachi 3:8)*

"Bring the whole tithe into the storehouse, that there may be food in my house. Test me in this, says the LORD Almighty, and see if I will not throw open the floodgates of heaven and pour out so much blessing that there will not be room enough to store it." (Malachi 3:10)

"On the first day of every week each one of you should set aside a sum of money in keeping with his income, saving it up , so that when I come no collections will have to be made." (1 Corinthians 16:2)

"Each man should give what he has decided in his heart to give, not reluctantly or under compulsion, for God loves a <u>cheerful giver</u>." (2 Corinthians 9:7)

*"Give, and it will be given to you.
A good measure, pressed down,
shaken together and running
over, will be poured into your lap.
For with the measure you use, it
will be measured to you."
(Luke 6:38)*

Living God's Word, loving, giving, tithing doesn't guarantee the day you accept Him this amazing bounty from Heaven with everything you've ever wanted will fall at your feet. This is not a ***"get rich quick"*** scheme. You can't buy God's love. It means when we accept Him and trust Him, He is going to love us like we love our own children, and provide for us as we provide for our own children. When He knows your heart for Him, He will supply all your needs:

His Word:

> *"And my God will supply all your
> `needs according to His riches in
> glory in Christ Jesus."
> (Philippians 4:19)*

And, just as we provide for the needs of our children, we don't always give them **"all"** that they ask, when they ask. Not all that they ask for is in their best interest. As parents, we want what is best at the right time. God knows what is best for us. He knows the right time. BE PATIENT.

MY STORY – Note 6

The tithe...we are so greedy! How much do we spend on non-essential things every day of the week? Restaurants, entertainment, recreation, novelties?

I absolutely knew from past experiences that during my worst times, when in church, I felt led to just empty my purse into the offering plate, put in my last $20, not knowing what I would feed my children for dinner. And, for some crazy reason, we ALWAYS had a great dinner! How does that work??? God's Plan!

Once I knew about the tithe, I decided to actually "test" Him with my earnings. Since that day, I have never stopped tithing because He has

ALWAYS provided. This is my testimony! This is first hand experience.

Doors would open, a new opportunity would unfold before my eyes. Without a college education, no experience, I was offered a position with a national company to assist in their building of a beautiful 200,000 square foot retail development project on Hilton Head Island. Was this a dream or what?

I had been turned down after my initial interview with the owners. In my numerous employment ventures, I had managed a small retail center in Cleveland, definitely not enough experience for this project! They would look elsewhere. However, knowing that the developer wanted a local person to manage the project, I started thinking about how/what I could do to make them reconsider. I didn't know anything about large developments. I had only been on the island for six months so I didn't know anything about building, zoning, environment, codes, etc. Then, the Lord gave me a word:

His Word:

"Whatever you do, work at it with all your heart, as working for the Lord, not for human masters."
Colossians 3:23-24

What could I do? Pray for wisdom. The Holy Spirit led me to continue communicating with the developer over several months: just sending them information, local newspaper updates of island activity, environmental issues, development, current projects, etc. (I had never considered doing anything like this before...it was His wisdom and guidance); educating myself as I educated them.

Six months later (patience)...collecting unemployment and preparing for that next move), I received an offer from the developer with an unbelievable salary. Were my storehouses overflowing? Or, what? God's Plan!

They liked my ingenuity, creativity and commitment. In addition, the company proceeded to train me at various universities around the country (Michigan State, Arizona State, University of Illinois, to name a few) for classes in retail development, management, marketing, leasing. An education that changed my life. Opportunities unfolded. God is so, so good! Just trust Him. He has the plan and it's not always on our time schedule. Have patience. It's His Plan for the children He loves.

"Unfortunately, many people are not livng in God's highest and best. They are not enjoying God's great plans and they are not experiencing the abundant life. There is a really good reason for that. Sin."

Beth Jones
Pastor & Author
The Basics With Beth

CHAPTER 6

HEALING

What if you saw an advertisement for a new product that could heal and remove ALL pain and disease? Would you want to run out and purchase that product?

Just now in the Year 2020, our nation is confronting the worst pandemic most of us will ever experience, corona virus, Covid19. When do we ever recall seeing our friends and neighbors, daring to veer out of their homes with face coverings and masks just to buy food. Our nation's governors are imposing strict restrictions on our coming and going, businesses closed to the public and social distancing eliminating hugs and emotional support to our families.

We can never know when tragedy will strike, when cancer might invade our bodies, hearts may fail, or another virus will attack our families, our country.

Christ is the same today, tomorrow and forever. What He did then, He will do now. He did not need to be living among the sick, He only needed to speak the words.

His Word:

> *"And the prayer of faith shall save the sick, and the Lord shall raise him up and if he has sinned, they shall forgive him. Confess your faults one to another, and pray one to another, that ye may be healed." (James 5:15)*

> *"And He Himself bore our sins in His body on the cross, so that we might die to sin and live to Righteousness; for by His wounds you were healed." (Isaiah 53:5)*

"Worship the Lord your God, and His blessing will be on your food and water. I will take away sickness from among you."
(Exodus 23:25)

"But I will restore you to health and heal your wounds, declares the Lord." (Jeremiah 30:17)

Jesus went about his ministry performing many miracles of healing. Saul of Tarsus, who had murdered many followers of Christ and was on a mission to persecute more and arrest them, lost his eyesight when Jesus appeared to Him in a great light. Obeying Christ's instructions, three days later his vision was restored. Saul had seen the power of Jesus. He experienced a total conversion, came to be known as Paul, Christ's disciple, who went about preaching that Jesus was the son of God.

There are so many other examples recorded, i.e., the beggar who had been born blind, healing the official's son without ever seeing him, the man with leprosy, the young daughter brought back to life, the woman with the issue of blood who only touched his garment and was healed.

So many witnessing and seeing his healing the word spread and they followed and crowds gathered and they **believed.**

His Word:

> *"They brought to Him all that were ill, those suffering various diseases and pains, demoniacs, epileptics, paralytics, and he healed them." (Matthew 4:24)*

> *"Great crowds came to him, bringing the lame, the blind, the crippled, the mute and many others, and laid them at his feet and he healed them."*
> *(Matthew 15:30)*

"Well," you might say, *"all these stories and healings/miracles were done a long time ago, and have been told many times over by many people. How do 'we' know in this day and age that God still heals and performs miracles?"*

Maybe you should speak to the father of an 18 month old daughter who hung upside down in a totally submerged car for 12 hours in frigid waters. Rescuers were led by a voice that to this day no one has accounted for.

Or, just research the word *"miracles"* and your pages will be full of God's hand in so many unexplainable healings.

More recently, there have even been movies featuring true stories of God's miraculous happenings.

Our faith comes from **"hearing"** and believing (not seeing) the Word of God. Faith is believing without seeing because we trust God's Word.

His Word:

>*"Consequently, faith comes from hearing the message, and the message is heard through the word about Christ." (Romans 10:17)*

>*"Go," said Jesus, "your faith has healed you." Immediately he received his sight and followed Jesus along the road." (Mark 10:52)*

>*"Then Jesus answered and said unto her, O woman, great is thy faith: be it unto thee even as thou wilt. And her daughter was made whole from that very hour." (Matthew 15:28)*

>*"You don't have enough faith," Jesus told them. "I tell you the truth, if you had faith even as small as a mustard seed, you could say to this mountain,*

'Move from here to there,' and
it would move. Nothing would
be impossible." (Matthew 17:20)

"But they that wait upon the
LORD shall renew their strength;
they shall mount up with wings as
eagles; they shall run, and not be
weary; and they shall walk, and
not faint." (Isaiah 40:31)

MY STORY – Note 7

God's healing touch is not always for physical needs but also emotional. Leaving my dysfunctional childhood, I spent the next 25 years in a dark place that the devil had created for my life; bad choices, divorces, financial struggles, etc. My three beautiful daughters were my blessing during those times. But, when my relationship with Christ began to develop, it was as if the scales had been removed from my eyes.

We all know the stories of Christ's miraculous healings of the blind, the paralytic, the raising of the dead.

We hear of miracles every day. There are testimonies of children who have been near death, experienced Heaven and yet returned to their overwhelmed parents. Innocent children with accounts and specifics that cannot be explained.

A few years ago we heard the story of a young 4 year old girl, Akiane Kramarik, who had a near death experience. She described in great detail her encounter with Jesus and Heaven. By age 6 she was consumed by her desire to paint a portrait of the face of Jesus as she remembered. She completed the painting by age 8. She had to use a step ladder for the 4' tall painting. Her story and beautiful likeness of Jesus Christ (as we think that he may look) have been publicized many times and resulted in her appearance on numerous international venues. No one can explain her unique experience.

I believe that we are living a miracle today through my grandson who loved sports, for three years he had played ice hockey and loved it. Only 7 at the time, but our family always felt that he would be a big guy, definitely sports material. Two years ago, a rare disease attacked his body resulting in acquired heart disease. Aneurysms in his coronary arteries meant restricted childhood activities, no contact sports and a lifetime of blood thinners. Levi was placed on numerous church prayer lists in various states. He is in our prayers daily and we are believing for complete and whole recovery. Last year at his one year anniversary of the diagnosis, we were told that the aneurysms are shrinking. His doctor's comment was "amazing!" His case is atypical, recovery rare in children over five.

We are coming upon his annual evaluation again, we stand in agreement that we will hear miraculous results that will mystify the physicians. And, we may not get our answer today or at the next test but that does not mean that our faith will waiver. We will be patient. We will pray and believe.

God's got this! And, His plan for Levi will is better than we could ever dream!

Our Savior heals our pain and suffering, replaces our mental anguish with positive attitude; difficult memories, with Hope; and stress, with His peace.

"Thinking faith thoughts, and speaking faith words, will lead the heart out of defeat and into victory."

Kenneth E. Hagin
Author & Evangelist
Word of Faith Movement

CHAPTER 7

ETERNITY

What if you knew that one day you would be face to face with God and Jesus at his right hand?

What if God had actually forgiven AND forgotten every sin you had ever committed?

What if you knew for certain, that you would one day live in Heaven with God! Jesus! Your loved ones who have gone before you (your spouse, your child, your parents), and behold their beautiful faces again? Would you grasp that opportunity?

Why do we need God? Why do we want to go to Heaven? Heaven is God's dwelling place.

In the Bible it is referred to as the new Jerusalem:

A crystal-clear river will flow between the throne of God and the Lamb (Jesus). The streets will be like pure gold and walls of the city will be covered with every kind of jewel and stone, beautiful flowers and trees of every kind. Light will come from the Lord's presence.

We read that there will be angels singing. When Jesus was on the cross, he referred to it as Paradise.

We need God because He loves us, He provides for us, He protects us, He heals us, He gives us hope, He died for us...so that one day we might have eternal life with Him in Heaven.

His Promises:

*"I will rescue him, I will protect
him, I will answer him, I will be
with him in time of distress, I will
deliver him, I will honor him (to
make rich, strong), long life will
satisfy him, I will show him my
salvation, deliverance and victory."
(Psalms 91:14-16)*

*"I am he who blots out your
transgressions for my own sake,
and I will not remember your
sins." (Isaiah 43:25)*

*Then He adds, "I will remember
their sins and lawless deeds no
more." (Hebrews 10:17)*

How comforting to know that when we take
our last breath, we will join our Heavenly
Father in a final resting place, Paradise. True,
and even though most of us have not
experienced or witnessed its beauty. God,

through His prophets, apostles, and disciples has given us an idea of what is to come.

And, He has told us...

His Word:

> *"But now they desire a better country, that is, an heavenly: wherefore God is not ashamed to be called their God: for he hath prepared for them a city."*
> *(Hebrews 11:16)*

> *"Do not let your hearts be troubled. Trust in God; trust also in me. In my Father's house are many rooms; if it were not so, I would have told you. I am going there to prepare a place for you. And if I go and prepare a place for you, I will come back and take you to be with me that you also may be where I am."*
> *(John 14:1-3)*

"For God so loved the world that he gave his one and only Son, that whoever believes in him shall not perish but have eternal life." John 3:16)

"Jesus answered, 'I am the way and the truth and the life. No one comes to the Father except through me." (John 14:6)

"In reply Jesus declared, 'I tell you the truth, no one can see the kingdom of God unless he is born again.'" (John 3:3)

"That if you confess with your mouth, 'Jesus is Lord,' and believe in your heart that God raised him from the dead, you will be saved." (Romans 10:9)

This is a place where we will meet Jesus, face to face. We will bow down in awe of Him. Our names will be read from the Lambs Book of

Life. We will praise His name. He will walk among us and every tear will be wiped from our eyes. He will remove all pain or mourning. Loved ones who have gone before us will be there for our embrace and Christ will make everything new.

Why would anyone NOT want to believe that there is an afterlife? How comforting is it to think that our loved ones are dropped into a hole to rot and decay and be no more. That's all there is??? How beautiful to know that we will go to paradise with Jesus and behold the faces of those we loved.

Lee Strobel wrote a book called "*The Case For Christ*". He was an atheist with a Master of Studies in Law degree from Yale and worked as the legal editor for the *Chicago Tribune*, an investigative journalist. So much of his work involved criminal cases, some with only circumstantial evidence used to charge, judge and imprison? Circumstantial evidence only... and yet with all the proof we have of Christ, many still doubt His existence. It is not even circumstantial.

We have actual evidence!

When Strobel's wife became a Christian,...He thought she had lost her mind. Strobel set out to "prove" that it was all a grand hoax. He was an investigative reporter for one of the largest newspapers in America. He could put a stop to this myth. He was certain there was no evidence that Jesus of Nazareth really was the Son of God.

His journey included interviews with a dozen of this world's greatest biblical scholars from Cambridge, Princeton, and other prestigious institutions, including other skeptics. He researched historical evidence, scientific (archeological) evidence, and psychiatric evidence of Christ's claims to be the Son of God.

His interviews asked the hard questions trying to disprove Jesus Christ. Strobel's riveting quest led him to Christianity! He has been interviewed on numerous national television programs including ABC's 20/20, Fox News and CNN. He became a teaching pastor of

Willow Creek Community Church in South Barrington, Illinois, from 1987 to 2000 before shifting his focus to writing and producing his TV show, Faith Under Fire.

In addition, for those looking for evidence, there are numerous recent true stories, books and movies of personal experiences telling of seeing God, Jesus, Heaven, Hell and the afterlife.

Today's Events of Christ's Existence:

Heaven Is Real BOOK/MOVIE
Colton Burpo, 4 year old who suffered burst appendix and multiple complications, coma. Doctors didn't expect his survival but he did recover. Some time later he began telling his parents about strange events, describing Heaven and people he saw and talked to who had passed and that he had no way of knowing.

I Am With You Always
Book by Perla Apolonio of her supernatural encounter with Jesus.

23 Minutes In Hell
Book by Bill Wiese of his personal experience of losing 23 minutes of his life where he experienced the tortures of hell.

Akaine Kramarik – The Girl Who Paints Heaven Movie
Born to atheist parents, 4 year old Akaine began having visions of Christ and Heaven. She began her first painting of Jesus at four. She is world renowned.

40 Days In Heaven
Book/Seneca Sodi gives testimony of her visit to the Holy City, Paradise and God's throne.

Tortured In Hell, Lived to Tell
YouTube Professional man addicted to drugs has out of body experience, stepping outside the body, looking down on his hospital experience. Six months later planned suicide. The night before his suicide he experienced the screams of hell, smells, torture. Became a Christian.

MY STORY – Note 8

I've often wondered what that day will be like when we see Jesus face to face. Or, what if He just appeared in our path unexpectedly one day? Falling to our knees in reverence, could we even speak or want to? He is so worthy of our praise. Sometimes we forget that He is always with us "every day." He lives in us. We should always glorify Him.

My wonderful Mother lived to be 93. I once mentioned to her that she is one of the few people I knew who had never lost a child, even at her old age. What a blessing! We typically assume that we will not outlive our children but that is not always the case. I have several friends who have experienced that terrible loss with their babies, children, teenagers and their mature sons and daughters. I am thankful, as of today, God has spared me. But, if that were to happen, I can't imagine going through life without any hope, without any peace, without God's plan for the hereafter and not knowing that we would be reunited again with our loved one.

I look forward to the day when I can embrace my beautiful mother again in Heaven, see the happiness on her face and know the joy and peace she has been given through Christ Jesus.

There is a battle with satan that rages against all who love the Lord. A battle that is won when we deny Christ, when we think we can "wait" a little longer, look the other way until "we're" ready for all that Christianity stuff, i.e., maybe when we're older like our parents. Time is not always our friend.

"All old people become Christians, right?" Maybe, we see it in the older generations because of what they've lived through, the struggles they have endured, the loses they have experienced. They finally caved to a Higher Power!

Maybe, they have just realized that we can enjoy ALL of God's blessings today; blessings greater than your own imagination. Don't waste precious years of blessings for you and your children. Don't wait until the end when you want to be certain you make it to Heaven. We all want *better for our children than what we had, just like our Heavenly Father wants for his children. We will ALL see Him face to face one day:*

He has told us one day we will all stand before Him.

His Word:

> *"[8]And being found in human form, he humbled himself by becoming obedient to the point of death, even death on a cross. [9]Therefore God has highly exalted him and bestowed on him the name that is above every name, [10]so that at the name of Jesus every knee should bow, in heaven and on earth and under the earth, [11]and every tongue confess that Jesus Christ is Lord, to the glory of God the Father." Philippians 2:8-11*

MY STORY – Note 9

I want to share the salvation of my earthly father and his journey to Eternity with Christ. We never knew exactly where dad stood. Our father was an angry, insecure man and, we believe, much of his unhappiness and difficulties were due to mental illness. After we were all grown, occasionally he would go to church with our mother. Dad would not take communion and never confessed Jesus as his Lord and Savior. A stoic person like him would never surrender anything to anyone.

In his later years he developed terminal health issues, was hospitalized, and placed in hospice. When I received the call and boarded the plane to come home, my seat assignment was between two pastors returning from a mission trip. We talked about my father's illness and his lack of faith. They prayed intensely with me for my father's salvation twice during the flight. My home church family was praying as well.

The night of his death, we experienced the fiercest thunderstorm I have ever known. I knew so many Christians were praying for my father's spirit that night. As I attempted to drive back to the hospital where my brother was sitting with my dad, the storm became so intense, piercing lightning, earthshaking thunder, roads flooding, I had to pull over to the side of the road. It was at that time that I could see the battle raging in the clouds between satan and God for my father's soul. I prayed profusely and screamed at satan, "you can't have him," "you can't have him," as the lightning slashed the dark clouds. The battle raged on, I prayed on! My eyes were filled with tears when I finally was able to get back on the road. I arrived at the hospital in pouring rain but the storm was ceasing.

My brother met me in the doorway of our father's room, telling me that all the power had gone out at the hospital, the generators had not kicked on and the staff had been in a panic. My brother is a Pastor. He, too, realizing the battle that was raging. held our father's hand and prayed like he had never prayed before. It was then as he asked our dad to accept Christ, that he felt our father's hand tighten in acceptance, his eyes fluttered open for the last time. Friends of my brother told us later that they had stood on their front porch during that stormy battle, also, praying for our father's salvation. We know now for certain that he, too, is in Heaven with Christ Jesus, our mother, and all his loved ones. We know that the power of satan that had doomed his entire earthly life is forever bound. We know that one day we will see him in Heaven and see the countenance of God and His peace upon our father's face that he could never find in this world. What a day that will be!

"Satan's greatest success is in making people think they have plenty of time before they die to consider their eternal welfare."

John Owen
Theologian
University of Oxford

CHAPTER 8

THE COUNSELOR

What if you were given an invisible mentor, advisor, or counselor; someone who could impart to you untold wisdom and guidance in every aspect of your life. He would live with you every minute of every day to help you make the perfect decisions for your life, your family, your work?

Would you welcome that expertise?

The disciples were very concerned and sad the Christ had to go away, to die on the cross. He told them that He would send them a Comforter, Helper, an Advocate (Holy Spirit) to guide them. He said that if He did not leave, the Helper could not come, and it would be to their advantage to have the

Comforter. We know the Comforter as the Holy Spirit. When we accept Christ as our Savior, the Holy Spirit comes to dwell in us. The Holy Spirit is God living in us.

To some it may equate to our conscience. The Holy Spirit is there to give us wisdom, guidance, to teach us. He is always available, 24/7. The Holy Spirit, God, wants to have a relationship with you. He is there for you to have conversations, ask for His direction, rely on the wisdom He will impart if you are willing to open your heart and listen. The Holy Spirit has all the answers.

He will intercede for you when you cry out to God. He is your *"best friend"* when you need someone to talk to. He will let you know when you are going astray and direct you to the right path. He will comfort you when there is no comfort to be found.

His Word:

> *"But I tell you the truth, it is to your advantage that I go away; for if I do not go away, the Helper will*

not come to you; but if I go, I will
send Him to you." (John 14:7)

"But the Helper, the Holy Spirit,
whom the Father will send in
My name, He will teach you all
things, and bring to your
remembrance all that I said
to you." (John 14:26)

"In certain ways we are weak,
but the Spirit is here to help us.
For example, when we don't
know what to pray for, the Spirit
prays for us in ways that cannot
be put into words." (Romans 8:26)

MY STORY – Note 10

When I look back upon my life, I marvel at where my journey with God has taken me. So many years plagued with strife and disappointment, I now experience His grace He is my Comforter. I just didn't know! The Holy Spirit who lives in me is my friend, my counselor, my advisor. We have a relationship. I go to him when I'm uncertain, confused, want to do the right thing, when I seek His peace. We talk, just like you and I would talk. I put my faith and confidence in the Holy Spirit. Sometimes the conclusion is not something I prefer but it is ALWAYS the right thing. He knows my heart, He is my Father, He loves me, He will never lead me astray.

Years after completing the development project on the resort island, married and just relocating to the state of Michigan, once again, it was time for a new employment opportunity. Being new to the area, having no connections, I took on three jobs to help with finances. One was a temporary position as a clerk, working in a small secretarial pool, filing invoices, $10/hr. No one knew my background, my prominent position with the retail developer, etc. Sixty days into the position, the local newspaper published an article that my employer had acquired a large downtown hotel and had plans to do a multi-million-dollar renovation.

They would need a retail floor in the hotel and were seeking someone with retail development experience to work on this part of the project.

Guess who was blessed with another miracle position? God put me in that place at that time. When times are difficult, we have to be willing to be responsible and sometimes face a little humility. Being humbled and accepting of a $10/hr salary opened doors that led to so much more.

His Word:

> **"Anyone who does not provide for their relatives, and especially for their own household, has denied the faith and is worse than an unbeliever." (1 Timothy 5:8)**

I feel like God's hand is always clinging to me, that He allows me to make my choices, but when I need Him, He just picks me up and places me where He wants me to be…and it is always a good, good thing! He leads me, He opens my eyes to opportunity, He gives me wisdom, He directs my path.

"You are extremely, totally loved by our Father. Breathing new life into your spirit has been His greatest victory. And He is very pleased with YOU."

Terry Prince
Pastor & Author
God's Family Church

CHAPTER 9

HOPE

What if? What if there was always something/someone you could reach out to, hold on to, to get you through the down times, the struggles, the depression and be able to ascribe to a positive, uplifting, overcomer attitude?

Would you take hold and never let go?

We use the word *"hope"* in so many ways. *"I hope this happens, I hope this, I hope that"*. What is hope? Webster's Dictionary says hope is: a desire accompanied by expectation of or belief in fulfillment. What would our life be without *"hope"*? Everything status quo, no way to overcome difficulties. Doom? Despair? Jesus promised us Hope! He tells us of His grace and His mercy and His good news plan for our life. Therefore, no matter what we face, whatever situation we go through, we can always have Hope and a positive outlook for tomorrow. Hope is eternal!

His Word:

> *"I pray that the eyes of your heart*
> *may be enlightened in order that*
> *you may know the HOPE to which*
> *He has called you, the riches of*
> *His glorious inheritance in His holy*
> *people and His incomparably great*
> *power for us who believe. That power*
> *is the same as the mighty strength*
> *He exerted when He raised Christ*
> *from the dead and seated Him at*
> *His right hand in the Heavenly*
> *Realm." (Ephesians 1:18-20)*

> *"For I know the plans I have for*
> *you, declares the Lord, plans*
> *to prosper you and not to harm*
> *you, plans to give you hope and a*
> *future." (Jeremiah 29:11)*

*"May the God of HOPE fill you
with all joy and peace. In believing,
so that by the power of the Holy Spirit
you may abound in HOPE."
(Romans 15:13)*

*"In the HOPE of Eternal Life,
which God, who does not lie,
promised before the beginning
of time." (Titus 1:2)*

Remember Joseph, the one with the beautiful multi-colored robe? He was despised by his brothers, tossed into a pit, sold into slavery, accused of rape, thrown into prison. But Joseph never lost hope in God. He had God's favor and God had the ultimate plan for Joseph's life: The plan to make him Pharaoh's chief administrator of Egypt; the plan for Joseph to prosper and be in good health.

Maybe you feel life is all disappointment. Maybe you feel broken! I remember walking on the beach, shelling, with my 5-year-old granddaughter as she picked up every shell along the way, even the *"broken"* ones. When I suggested she only pick up the pretty, unbroken pieces, her reply was, *"They're all beautiful to me, Grandma."* (Be still my heart!) If we could only see through the innocent eyes of children. We are all beautiful to God. He gave us Hope through Jesus Christ!

God walked Moses, Joseph and David through the difficulties, the despair, the hardship right into a place of prominence and power. It didn't *"just happen"*. It was God's plan. He has a plan just for you! Cling to your faith. Cling to your hope.

MY STORY – Note 11

"Eternal life" means life forever, life, even after death, living with Jesus in Heaven. It is that Hope of Eternal Life that gives us peace as our lives come to an end. We know that Heaven will be more amazing than we could ever imagine, more beautiful than anything we have ever known. We know that we will see Jesus face to face. We know

that when we lose our loved ones, we find comfort in knowing that one day we will look upon their beautiful faces again.

I remember three years ago when a dear couple, friends of ours, lost their only daughter and their two-year old grandchild. They were murdered by the husband/father. What could ever be more devastating? Evil, pain and sorry are not of God. I remember the horror I felt, the empathy for this dear family. I had to excuse myself to gain composure.

We sat with them and listened as they shared with us how their life had fallen apart in the matter of a few weeks, how their hearts had been ripped out, how their lives had been changed forever. (I pray to God that you never have that experience.)

As they continued, I saw two people who were leaning on God's promises. We heard them give thanks to God for the peace that His Word was bringing to them. We heard them thank God for the time these loved ones had been a part of their lives. We listened as they spoke of HOPE and encouragement they received from God's Word and God's promises of eternal life. Yes, they were hurt.

Yes, they were grieving their loss. Yes, they would have bad days ahead. Yet, they "knew" without a doubt that their loved ones were in a beautiful, wonderful place in the care of Jesus. They "knew" that their loved ones would never experience hurt and pain ever again. They "knew" that one day they would be with them again in Heaven. Without their trust in God, how could anyone have the strength to overcome such pain?

How does anyone get through life's difficulties? What if we didn't have God's Word, His promises, His Son, His forgiveness, His plan for our lives? How would we *"know"* what happens when we leave this world? We would have nothing without His Word, the Bible.

Why do so many wait until they have a crisis in their life, until they are on their knees, begging God, someone, anyone for help? He is always there! He is waiting.

He is peace. He is comfort. He is HOPE.

CHAPTER 10

GOD VS. SATAN -- GOOD VS. EVIL

Is there really a big, bad bogeyman lurking among us that is called satan? Really? Come on now?!!

The answer is **"yes"**. Just as we have to **"believe"**, without seeing, in Jesus Christ.

We must also believe that the evil one walks among us. God has told us that. He was created before the world began. He was created by God as the guardian cherub. He was in a place of honor...but his beauty and pride, his desire to be greater than God was his downfall. He appears as a serpent in the Garden of Eden.

His Word:

> *"You were blameless in our ways*
> *from the day you were created;*
> *till unrighteousness was found*
> *in you. In the abundance of your*
> *trade you were filled with violence*
> *in your midst, and you sinned;*
> *I cast you as a profane thing*
> *from the mountain of God, and*
> *I destroyed you, O guardian*
> *cherub, from the midst of the*
> *stones of fire. You were anointed*
> *guardian cherub. Your heart was*
> *proud because of your beauty;*
> *you corrupted your wisdom for*
> *the sake of your splendor. I*
> *cast you to the ground; I exposed*
> *you before kings."*
> *(Ezekiel 28:15-17)*

The Garden of Eden was created by God as the most perfect, beautiful abode for his creation, Adam and Eve. God created these beings to fellowship with Him, to have a relationship with Him. People ask, *"If God is so good, why does he deprive us of things?"* *"Why doesn't He just make everything 'perfect'?"* The answer is He did!

He gave us everything in the Garden of Eden.

There was only one restriction: Not to eat from the Tree of Knowledge, also known as the Tree of Good and Evil. Adam and Eve had no reason to defy God. They only needed to know that their Creator had given them everything they could ever desire. But, they made a decision, a choice without including God. ***"Their way"*** When they took the first bite of the apple, Adam and Eve came to know evil. The same evil that exists today.

His Word:

> *"Now war arose in heaven,*
> *Michael and his angels fighting*
> *against the dragon. And the*
> *dragon and his angels fought back,*
> *but he was defeated, and there*

*was no longer any place for them
in heaven. And the great dragon
was thrown down, that ancient
serpent, who is called the devil
and satan, the deceiver of the
whole world – he was thrown down
to the earth; and his angels were
thrown down with him."
(Revelation 12:7-9)*

The evil one, in an attempt to discredit God, enticed Eve to eat of that tree. They were no longer God's perfect creation. Their eyes were opened to *"worldly"* things. We live in that *"world"* today with satan, the spirit of the air, lucifer, evil one, the adversary, etc. He is the ruler of this world. Adam and Eve allowed satan to destroy their relationship with God, just as many of us do today.

His Word:

*"We know that we are from God,
and the whole world lies in the
power of the evil one."
(1 John 5:19)*

When Christ walked this earth, satan even tempted Him. He is a powerful force, yet today.

Anyone can be tempted.

His Word:

> *"Then, Jesus was led by the spirit into the wilderness to be tempted by the devil."*
> *(Matthew 4:1)*

> *"Again, the devil taketh him up into an exceeding high mountain, and sheweth Him all the kingdoms of the world, and the glory of them. And saith unto him, All these things will I give thee, if thou will fall down and worship me. Jesus said to him, "Away from me, satan. For it is written, Worship the Lord your God and serve Him only. Then, the devil left him and the angels came and attended him."*
> *(Matthew 4:8-11)*

When we do not believe and accept Jesus Christ, we cannot be under God's protection.

We are open to the continued destruction by satan, who comes to steal, kill and destroy. His only goal is to destroy our beautiful relationship with God. He delights every time he hears, *"Why did God do that?"*, *"Where is God?"*, *"God must hate me"*, *"How can a good God let these things happen?"*

So often we are eager to blame our circumstances, finances, marriage difficulties, issues with children on God.

Where does this come from?

People turn their back on God, do not accept Him, deny Him…yet, when there are problems, they blame Him, someone they don't even recognize is in existence.

Yep, that is a GOOD day for satan!! You have made his day!

His Word:

*"The god of this world has blinded
the minds of the unbelievers, to
keep them from seeing the light of
the gospel of the glory of Christ,
who is the image of God."
(2 Corinthians 4:4)*

Even when we forget, Jesus is always near, waiting for you to answer His call...just waiting to give you hope, good health, a beautiful future and eternal life (All the things He promises)...so is the evil one, lurking nearby to bring you to your knees, rip out your heart, destroy your life.

His Word:

*"The thief comes only to steal,
kill and destroy. I have come that
they might have life and have it
abundantly." (John 10:10)*

We all have days where everything seems to go wrong, running late to an appointment, kids missed the school bus, you didn't get that pay raise, your spouse has strayed, you burned dinner, your mom or dad has been diagnosed with a fatal illness!
His Word:

> *"And they may come to their senses and escape from the snare of the devil, captured by him to do his will." (2 Timothy 2:26)*

My response to his evil will in my life:

> **"Not today, satan! I'm not going there! You will not steal my joy!"**

Jesus gives us strength and courage to stand up to satan, to defy his efforts to ruin our day, RUIN OUR LJVES. Christ overcame the cross!

We believe; therefore, we are over comers! We have His Word, His promises, His love. We are His children. We are over comers!

How do you care for your children? Do you share your wisdom with them, do you protect them, do you do everything you can to give them a good life, do you love them?

"We" are God's children. He loves us. He is always there for us. You are never alone.

His Word tells us how to over come the evil of satan. He tells us that satan exists, that the evil one is lingering, always eagerly awaiting opportunities to bring us defeat. Only when we have a strong relationship with our Heavenly Father, when we know His Word, His weapon to over come evil, can we over come satan's evil will in our life.

God has promised to turn those things meant for evil, to good!

His Word:

> *"What you (satan) meant for evil,*
> *God will turn to good."*
> *(Genesis 50:20)*

We have witness of Christ's many miracles, converting and healing Saul's (Paul) vision, the paralyzed man at Capernaum, the woman with internal bleeding, bringing the daughter of a synagogue leader back to life, bringing life back to his beloved Lazarus, removing demons from a demonic man, healing lepers, feeding the 5,000 with only 5 small loaves and 2 fish, only to name a few.

We have witness of His resurrection from death on the cross. He lived then; He lives today. He did miracles then; He does miracles now.

Why do you hesitate?

His Word:

*"You used to live in sin, just
like the rest of the world, obeying
the devil – the commander of
the powers in the unseen world.
He is the spirit at work in the
hearts of those who refuse to
obey God." (Ephesians 2:2)*

*"...the simple are killed by
their turning away, and the
complacency of fools destroys
 them." (Proverbs 1:32)*

*"And, on turning away once
saved, For it had been better for
them not to have known the
way of righteousness, than, after
they have known, to turn from
the holy commandment
delivered unto them."
(2 Peter 2:21)*

"Like it or not, there's a spiritual battle raging right now for your heart and mind. As you think in your heart is the way that you'll be. Your thoughts become what you say and do, with your actions being the greatest expression of your authority. Therefore, you'll be influenced, dominated, and ruled by whomever you yield yourself to - God or Satan."

Andrew Wommach
TV Evangelist & Author
The Believer's Authority

CHAPTER 11

UNBELIEVERS

Spiritual Blindness

As the scriptures say, it is the intent of satan to steal, kill and destroy, to misguide and misinform so that Christ is denied and rejected. That is his only goal.

Often other Christians are Christ's own enemy, as they profess to be a Christian, yet their example is seriously flawed. Although, we know that we can never be perfect and we will make mistakes, others should always **"see"** Christ in us; in our attitude, our actions. When we fail, which may be often, we have to repent and ask His forgiveness, which He always gives. Knowing Christ helps our eyes to be open to our mistakes, our failures, and recognize that He is always there when we ask forgiveness.

Wars and killing have been carried out by those who would claim to be Christian. Christians are not perfect people. They can be led by other influences, emotions. That's why we NEED Christ! Without Him, we could all be loose cannons. Always letting our feelings/ emotions dictate our actions.

Nowhere in the bible does it say that we should bow down to evil, to those who would harm or rob us. The misnamed Christian Crusades were led mostly by non-Christians. The name of Christ was abused, misused and blasphemed by many during the Crusades. The purpose of the Crusades was to retake land from the Muslims who had invaded Israel, Jordan, Egypt, Syria and Turkey, previously occupied by Christians. The Muslims brutally oppressed, enslaved, deported and murdered the Christians. The Catholic Church, and some barbaric kings and emperors ordered the Christians to reclaim what was taken. In doing so, Muslims were forced to covert to *"Christianity"*. If they refused, they would be put to death in the name of Jesus Christ. There is no biblical justification for conquering lands, murdering civilians and destroying cities. These wars were A.D. 200-900.

Fortunately, we don't live in the past but we learn from the past. Even today, in wartimes, Christians will have to fight when our country or one of our allies is threatened. To deal with the issues of war crimes internationally, in 1864 the Geneva Convention Treaties were adopted along with the Hague Treaties to specify the rules of warfare and comprehensive protections for humanitarian law. The Treaties have been revised and expanded numerous times over the years.

Even though we can call ourselves Christian, we are also human. Any Christian who believes he is above making mistakes, bad decisions and breaking God's laws does not even understand why Christ went to the cross. Our sins are so great that He atoned for us! We can only know His will, and strive every day to live our lives in a way that honors Him.

We will all fail....but Christ forgives. He knows our heart! When we ask and repent, He hears.

His Word:

> *"And a voice came from Heaven saying, This is my Son in whom my soul is well pleased. I will put my spirit upon Him and He shall shew judgement upon the Gentiles." (Matthew 3:17)*

> *"Jesus said to him, 'I am the way, the truth and the life. No one come to the Father except through me." (John 14:6)*

> *"And without faith it is impossible to please Him, for whoever would draw near to God must believe*

that He exists, and that He
rewards those who seek Him."
(Hebrews 11:6)

If believing is so wonderful, why would anyone NOT want to accept Jesus Christ?

Why? Because it means giving up pride and control! It means admitting and accepting that there is something out there greater than YOU!!

Why not try it and see for yourself?

See yourself at peace even in the midst of difficulties.

See how what you now have becomes more than enough.

See the lives of your children blessed.
See your marriage become grounded and fall in love again.

See doors opened and opportunities come through.

See strongholds in your life broken forever.

Always, have someone to talk to.

MY STORY – Note 12

I have lived them all! I speak from my own personal experience! We are to be a testimony for Him, to share our faith, not to be ashamed of our failures but to give Him glory for the successes we've witnessed in our own lives. We're to be like excited little children telling others of His goodness.

I remember singing "Jesus Loves Me" to my 3-year-old granddaughter at bedtime a few years ago, "we are weak, but He is strong", then explaining how Jesus knew her before she was ever born and the number of hairs on her head, how much He loves her and protects her.

As I stepped away for a moment, returning, I stopped in the doorway to hear her sweet little voice explaining to her 18-month-old brother in her own innocent interpretation, "He is only this big," as she pinched her tiny fingers together (misinterpreting the "little" used in the song) "but He's very strong. He knows how many hairs you have. He loves you. He will keep you safe." Innocence, honest glory to God!

His Word: (regarding Unbelievers)

> **"They are darkened in their understanding, alienated from the life of God because of the ignorance that is in them, due to their hardness of heart." (Ephesians 4:18)**

> **"In their case, the god of this world (satan), has blinded the minds of the unbelievers, to keep them from seeing the light of the gospel of the glory of Christ, who is the image of God." (2 Corinthians 4:4)**

"For the wages of sin is death, but the free gift of God is Eternal life in Christ Jesus, our Lord." (Romans 6:23)

"He who rejects me and does not accept my words; the very words I have spoken will condemn them at the last day." (John 12:48)

"Then they will go to eternal punishment, but the righteous to eternal life." (Matthew 25:46)

"They will be punished with everlasting destruction and shut out from the presence of the Lord and from the glory of his might." (2 Thessalonians 1:9)

"Then he will say to those on his left, 'Depart from me, you cursed, into the eternal fire prepared for the devil and his angels." (Matthew 7:23)

CHAPTER 12

FATHER, SON & HOLY SPIRIT

God created earth. He is our creator. He created everything your eyes can behold. God created humans for camaraderie, for His companionship. We are His family.

When Adam and Eve ate from the forbidden Tree of Knowledge in the Garden of Eden, their eyes were opened to *"worldliness."* They were no longer under God's perfect life plan in the Garden. They were now on their own. They had to reason for themselves. They had to make decisions. They had to work. They had to become responsible, just as we are today.

As time progressed and the earth became populated, God watched as His people made their choices: sinning, worshiping false gods, making bad choices. The world was flooded over by evil, corruption and violence.

God chose to send a flood of his own, destroying His own creation of mankind. Noah was the only follower of God left on the earth. He did everything just as God commanded. Noah and his family were spared to restart humanity. God made a covenant with Noah, that never again would the earth be destroyed by flood.

God watched His world develop and grow once again. People were obedient to God for a time. The purest of lambs were sacrificed as a sin offering to God for His forgiveness of their offenses against the religious laws of the land, and there were many.

> *"Then, God said "I desire*
> *steadfast love and not sacrifice,*
> *the knowledge of God rather*
> *than burnt offerings."*
> *(Hosea 6:6)*

So, God decided to send to earth a man, His son, Jesus, to live among His people, to walk His creation and make known God's love for mankind, His promises, His miracles, His peace and to save us from the wicked ways of mankind. He was sent to preach the good news of Salvation and Repentance. He was sent so that we might one day be received into God's kingdom. He was sent as our sin sacrifice once and for all.

Jesus led a pure, sinless life, born of a virgin. **700+/- years before His birth**, the Old Testament tells us of over 300 prophesies of the virgin birth, Jesus' life, sacrifice and resurrection long before they ever occurred.

His Word:

> *"Therefore, the Lord himself*
> *will give you a sign; The virgin*
> *will conceive and give birth to a*
> *son and will call him Immanuel."*
> *(Isaiah 7:14)*

*"O, Bethlehem Ephrathah, you
are but a small Judean village, yet
you will be the birthplace of my
King who is alive from everlasting
ages past." (Micah 5:2)*

Jesus experienced life on this earth just as we do. As a child He lived with his parents, Mary and Joseph. He worked as a carpenter, He was deeply loved by a woman, Mary, He was tempted by satan.

Jesus was loved and pursued by many who loved God. His words were received and believed! And, the crowds of followers continued to grow and expand.

As the evil rulers watched the acceptance of Jesus by the people, they began to fear His claim as *"King of the Jews"*. They feared the word *"King"*, as a threat to their authority and their control. The Messiah was prosecuted and condemned by his own people.

His Word:

> *"They have pierced my hands and feet." (Psalms 22:16)*

> *"Surely, he has borne our griefs and carried our sorrows; yet we esteemed him stricken, smitten by God and afflicted. But, he was pierced for our transgressions, he was crushed for our iniquities; upon him was the chastisement that brought us peace, and with his wounds we are healed."*
> *(Isaiah 53:4-5)*

Instead of each of us having to sacrifice for our own sins in life, instead of burnt offerings asking for forgiveness...this gentle pure lamb was beaten mercilessly, tortured and spat upon, and nailed to a cross (in our place). He bore **"our"** sins, He bore **"our"** pain, He bore **"our"** stripes. He is our forgiveness. All we have to do now is **" ask"**.

His Word:

"...For everyone, both great and small, shall really know me then, says the Lord, and I will forgive and forget their sins."
(Jeremiah 31:34)

Before his death and resurrection, Christ told his disciples and followers that it was best for them that He go away, but when he goes away, he would send a **"comforter"** who would never leave them. The comforter is the Holy Spirit (Jesus himself) who dwells within us today, when we accept Jesus Christ as Lord and Savior.

Father, Son and Holy Spirit, three in one, the Trinity.

CHAPTER 13

IF GOD IS A GOOD GOD, WHY DO WE HAVE SUFFERING?

There is a God.
There is evil.
There will always be God.
There will always be evil.

As long as we live on this earth, every day of our life we will have to make choices between good & evil.

Our omnipotent God gave man ALL authority over the earth when it was created.

His Word:

> *"In the beginning was the Word, and the Word was with God, and the Word was God...The Word became flesh and made*

his dwelling among us. We have seen his glory, the glory of the One and Only, who came from the Father, full of grace and truth." (John 1:1 & 14)

And, it was very, very good!

Through his deceit in the Garden of Eden, satan stole that authority from Adam and was cast down to earth.

His Word:

"How you have fallen from heaven, O morning star, son of the dawn! You have been cast down to the earth, you who once laid low the nations! You said in your heart, I will ascend to heaven; I will raise my throne above the stars of God; I will sit enthroned on the mount of assembly, on the utmost heights of the sacred mountain. I will ascend above the tops of the clouds; I will make myself like the

Most High." But you are brought down to the grave, to the depths of the pit." (Isaiah 14:12-15)

And evil arrived!

God came to earth in the image of man (Jesus), from the womb of a woman, born just as a small baby and grew up just as you and I. He had a mom and dad. He walked this sinful earth for 33 years to experience life on earth, to see the ways of man and to teach us how to live, how to love one another, how to know our Father in Heaven, to know His will for us, to guide us on a godly path, to give us hope, and to lead us to eternal life with God in Heaven.

Jesus saw evil. He saw corruption. He saw fear, lies and cruelty. He saw pain and suffering. He saw All of God's laws being broken. Man was doomed to burn in hell.

There was so much evil on this sinful earth that after Christ's three years of preaching, teaching, healing & performing miracles, it all came down to "suffering", to sacrifice!

Christ suffered! He was beaten down, spat upon, tortured beyond what any human man could survive....His hands and feet staked to a wooden cross, His body pierced, a human sacrifice (the unblemished lamb) to atone for ALL of man's sin! That's how bad our sin was.

A sin sacrifice so that **"we"**, God's people, would not have to be punished and our transgressions, God would forgive and forget.

That's what it took for us to be able to ask for God's forgiveness and acceptance and not to burn in hell; but to have hope, peace and eternal life after death in God's Kingdom..

Evil is still just as bad today! Probably worse! So many of God's laws are considered acceptable to our sinful world today. Our governments have even attempted to remove God completely. Could God make it all go away? Certainly, but, He's already done that. Remember the perfect, pure life in the Garden of Eden? Man made a bad choice and evil entered our world.

God had given man a brain, ability, intelligence. He gave man freedom and independence. Even with all that...man fell to temptation and brought evil into our world, sin. As long as we live in this world, we will know evil. We will always have to make choices. But Jesus is our bridge to God. When we confess our belief, His Holy Spirit comes to dwell in us giving us guidance, wisdom, hope. He brings us peace in whatever our circumstances.

If there were no evil, how would we know what *"evil"* is? How would we know what is good? How would be know good from evil? How would we know there is a satan out there who wishes to destroy us? A satan who wants to be god. Why would we *"need"* to know Jesus?

Jesus knew that He had to be sacrificed. He knew the horrific pain & torture His physical body would endure. He prayed to His Father until the sweat on His brow turned to blood to have another way, not this; but He was willing to do His Father's will.

Man needed to see, to experience first-hand just how much God loved this world, how much He would sacrifice just for you, for me, for mankind.

His Word:

> *"For God so loved the world that He gave His only begotten son that whosoever believeth in Him should not perish but have everlasting life." (John 3;16)*

After being beaten and dragged through the streets, Christ hung on the cross for 6 hours from 9 AM til 3 PM. Upon the cross, with his battered and torn body, twisted and broken, Jesus, the man, cried out, *"My God, my God, why have you forsaken me?"* At that moment, complete darkness covered the land!

In His pain and suffering, Jesus, our Savior, Son of God, prayed for his accusers, the Jews, Romans, sinners.

His Word:

> *"Father, forgive them. They know not what they do." (Luke 23:24)*

With His final agonizing breath, "It is finished," the darkened earth shook the ground, ripping the temple veil into from top to bottom, rocks split, and tombs broke open!

When the centurion and those with Him at the cross saw the force of the earthquake and all that had happened, they were terrified.

His Word:

> *"Truly, He is the Son of God!" (Matthew 27:54)*

But, God was not done yet! Man, also needed to see, to experience God's power. Man needed to know that the words God breathed to His prophets 700 years earlier and written in our bibles was alive and true.

Three days after Christ's body was entombed, and sealed with a mighty boulder by the Roman Empire guards, three female followers of Christ, coming to prepare Christ's body after death (as is the custom) found the boulder removed and an empty tomb. They were approached by two men in gleaming garments.

His Word:

> *"Why do you look for the living*
> *among the dead? He is not here,*
> *He is risen. Remember how He*
> *told you while He was still with you*
> *in Galilee, 'The Son of Man must be*
> *delivered over to the hands of sinners,*
> *be crucified and on the third day*
> *be raised again.'" (Luke 24: 5-7)*

The women hurried to_share the good news to the apostles.

Through God's power, Christ's resurrection and victory over death proves that Jesus is the Messiah. He was risen. He was alive. Following His resurrection, Jesus was seen by over 500 eyewitnesses, many who lived into the first century. If not true, Christ's disciples could have denied these events at any time and made considerable profit. They all spent the rest of their lives, praising and serving our Savior, Jesus Christ.

He is alive today. God is all powerful!

So back to our question, ***"If God is so good, why do we have suffering?"***

Because we live in a fallen world, a world where man was the overseer but then became satan's world, the world of sinful people. Unfortunately, we all sin every day. It is the inherent nature of man. Those who know God, believers, try to emulate the life of God, to be an example of His love and kindness.

Those who don't know God are left to their own devices, their own way. They are weak toward the temptations of the evil one. In their own frustration, pain, or depression they may take out their anger and weaknesses with cruelty and malice toward anyone and anything. They have no where to turn. Satan consumes them. People are hurt, people suffer. Good, kind people, even children, become their victims. Unbelievers have no hope. They have no peace.

No one could ever live up to God's standards. We could never be perfect, so our only hope is to confess our sins and ask for God's forgiveness, accepting Jesus, as the Son of God. We thank Him daily for all that He provides and pray for His blessings on our lives as we live in His grace and mercy until that day when He takes us to His perfect Kingdom in Heaven.

So we will always live with evil...but, we can find our peace through the hope of Jesus Christ that dwells within us.

Summary

There are so many unknowns in our world today. I guess that is true with every generation. Unknowns that are different from **"our way"** of life, things we question, things we just don't understand. When uncertainties occur, we often choose to put our heads in the sand, ignore the issue, or even become judgmental. Often, we have to step outside the box and think *"What would Jesus think of that?"* *"How should I react to things I don't understand?"* Three things Jesus is clear on: He loves us and we are all sinners. He forgives us, all of us daily. We are not to judge others. We are to love the way Jesus loves.

His Word:

> *"Do not judge, or you too will be judged. Why do you look at the speck of sawdust in your brother's eye and pay no attention to the plank in your own eye?" (Matthew 7:1-5)*

Jesus knows your heart. Jesus knows your thoughts. Maybe, you still can't believe that your sins can be forgiven??? He knows who you are. There is only **"one"** unpardonable sin.

His Word:

> *"Truly I say unto you, ALL sins*
> *will be forgiven the sons of men,*
> *and whatever blasphemes they*
> *may utter; but he who blasphemes*
> *against the Holy Spirit never has*
> *forgiveness, but is subject to eternal*
> *condemnation." (Mark 3:28-30)*

I ask myself, "*why wouldn't anyone give up everything they have today to live this beautiful, fulfilling life with ALL the blessings and benefits for the rest of their lives? Why would they continue to try and find their own way out of life's struggles, family issues, relationships, debt? Why?*"

Is it too difficult to just BELIEVE?

You have nothing to lose!

What is your priority?

You just don't have the time?
What TV series are you watching today?
How many hours of phone time?
Did you go to the gym?

You don't want to give up your social status?

Will your friends walk away?
You won't be invited to be with the "in" crowd?
You can't be the hit of the party?
You need that extra hour of sleep on Sunday?
You need to stay out late with your friends?
Those sporting events last too late?
You put in too many hours with work?
Sunday is our family day?

Maybe you have asked God to send help, to send solutions, to be there for you? Always *"asking, asking"*? And, nothing happened. You're still waiting...

Did you ever think to speak with Him when things were "*good*"?

Did you thank Him this morning for all the "*little*" things? Is the sky blue? Is the grass green? (The little things).

Do you let him know that you love Him and are grateful?

He knows who you are but does He know your voice?

His Word:

> **"Not everyone who says to me
> 'Lord, Lord', will enter the
> kingdom of Heaven but only
> the one who does the will of
> my Father who is in Heaven.
> Many will say to me that day,
> Lord, Lord, did I not prophesy
> in your name, did I not cast out
> demons in your name, did I not
> do many mighty works in**

your name. And, then I will
declare to them, 'I never
knew you.'" (Matthew 7:21-23)

I can guarantee you that when you accept Christ and set out to do His Word (**and that day will come),** you will look back and say, *"I just never knew life could be so good. I just didn't know! Why didn't someone tell me?"*

Can you come up with all the **how's** and **why's** of the blessings in my own personal life?

> - Why did I receive that call on a Sunday afternoon providing me with the career/education of a lifetime? Do bankers typically call people on Sunday afternoons?

> - Why was one of my first calls in the real estate world, the largest hospital in our area, who retained my services for the next 20 years?

- Why was I, new to the area and only 30 days into a $10/hr part time file clerk position, in the right place at the right time that the company acquired a hotel requiring developmental expertise that placed me in an executive position?

- Why was I the person answering phones the day a young pastor called for a small church facility? One, I have now served for over 25 years, participating in numerous real estate transactions (all purely miraculous) and watched them grow to over 3,000 members?

- Why did I find my perfect mate at a church?

- Why, after experiencing more than one divorce, do I have amazing, kind, moral children? They never used the *"divorce"* excuse.

-Why did my blessing of career successes and great health allow me at age 74 to become my company's Realtor of the Year as a woman in Commercial Real Estate & Development?

ALL occurred after I dedicated my life to Jesus Christ and began a personal relationship with Him!

It was not of me...He knows my voice! I wonder how it hurts His heart all the while standing there, waiting and watching, as you turn your back to Him, ignore Him, not make time for Him,...then, when your crisis comes, you scream out, *"God, help me! God, where are you. God, I need you!"*

Will He know who you are?

His Word:

> *"This is the confidence we have in approaching God, if we ask anything according to His will, He hears us." (1 John 5:14)*

"Therefore, whoever confesses Me before man, him, I will also confess before My Father, who is in heaven." (Matthew 10:32)

"In all your ways, acknowledge Him, and He will direct your path." (Proverbs 3:6)

You don't have enough time? I can assure you that when you take time for Him, your days will appear to be longer so you can experience more joy, your burden will become lighter, your needs will become smaller in comparison to your many blessings! God is a good, good Father!

Now, you can never say **"I didn't know"**.

How could anyone not want all the love and happiness Jesus has promised us?

All you have to do is say these words and believe:

Heavenly Father, I believe that Jesus Christ is your Son. I believe he died on the cross for my sins and rose again. I confess that I am a sinner and I ask your forgiveness. I declare that Jesus Christ is my Lord and Savior.

In Jesus name,
Amen

If you did say those words. If you meant those words. Please share your declaration with someone. Please find a good church where you can learn about His promises, honor Christ, show Him your love, your appreciation.

He is waiting...

If you enjoyed this book, I'd love to hear from you, joycewilesrealtor@gmail.com.

*"**Being** a Christian is more than just an instantaneous conversion - it is a daily process whereby you grow to be more and more like Christ."*

Billy Graham
American Evangelist

AUTHOR JOYCE P. WILES

Joyce Wiles is an author, realtor, wife, mother, and grandmother. She gives credit for her faith and love of Jesus Christ to her brother Pastor Terry Prince and Pastors Jeff and Beth Jones. Since Joyce dedicated her life to Jesus Christ, she tries to live each day in a way that honors Him.

Joyce's new book for teens, **Satan In My Head, Jesus In My Heart,** on the importance of having a relationship with Jesus and making good choices in life, starting today debuts fall of 2022! Satan is always finding ways to get into our head, even when we have Jesus in our heart. A strong foundation in faith will help teenagers fireproof the evils, temptations and confusion satan attempts to fire into their eyes, ears and head each and every day.

Joyce is available to speak to your church women's group, youth group, adult ministry or adult education workshops or conferences. To book Joyce to speak at an upcoming event you can email: joycewilesrealtor@gmail.com

DISCUSSION QUESTIONS FOR REFLECTION OR BIBLE STUDIES

Chapter 1: What If?

What is the price we pay for God's freedom? (Ephesians 2:8-9; Romans 11:6; Acts 13:38-39; Romans 8:1-2; 2 Corinthains 3:17; John 8:36 and 2 Timothy 1:9)

Chapter 2: God's Word – The Bible

Faith comes from hearing. How does the Bible help us to "hear" from God? (2 Timothy 3:16; Matthew 4:4; John 6:63 and Hebrews 4:12)

Chapter 3: Perfect Peace

How can a relationship with Christ affect your life? (John 3:16; Jeremiah 29:11; Ephesians 2:4-5; Matthew 11:28 and Exodus 35:31)

Chapter 4: Blessings I

What does being blessed with abundance mean? (2 Corinthians 9:8; Deuteronomy 28:12; James 1:27; Matthew 6:33; Philippians 4:19; Proverbs 3:10; Romans 15:130; Psalms 65:11 and Psalms 37:11)

Chapter 5: Blessings II

What are some examples of God's blessings in your life? (Micah 3:8-12; Matthew 6:21; Romans 12:1 and Proverbs 3:9-10)

Chapter 6: Healing

Do you know of anyone who has been healed by the mighty power of Jesus? (1 Peter 2:24; Matthew 9:35; Mark 5:34; James 5:14; 2 Kings 25:5; Matthew 11:28; James 5:15; Isaiah 53:5; Exodus 23:5; and Jeremiah 30:17)

Chapter 7: Eternity

What is the God's ultimate gift when we accept Jesus Christ as our Lord & Savior?
(Romans 6:23; John 10:28-30; 1 Peter 5:10; 1 John 2:17; 1 John 5:11; John 3:16; 1 Timothy 6:12 and Galatians 6:8)

Chapter 8: The Counselor

How does being filled with the Holy Spirit affect our lives throughout each & every day?
(John 14:26; Galatians 5:22-23; Galatians 31:3 and Romans 8:9-11)

Chapter 9: Hope

Hope means to cherish a desire with anticipation. What is your hope? (1 Peter 5:10; 1 Thessalonians 1:3; Colosians 1:27; Ephesians 1:8; Hebrews 10:23 and Isaiah 40:31)

Chapter 10: God vs Satan

How much power does satan have? (1 John 5:19; Romans 8:38-39; 1 Thessalonians 3:3; 2 Corinthians 10:4-5; 1 Peter 5:8-9; John 10:10; John 16:33; James 4:7 and 2 Corinthians 4:4)

Chapter 11: The Unbelievers

Is there really a hell? (Matthew 13:50; Proverbs 24:20; Ephesians 2:2; Revelation 21:8; Romans 13:4; Romans 12:2; John 14:6; 1 Corinthians 15:33; Revelation 10:10; Numbers 16:32-33; Matthew 25:41 and Matthew 13:42)

Chapter 12: Father, Son, Holy Spirit

Explain the Trinity, Godhead and why we need all three? (Isaiah 9:6; 2 Corinthians 13:14; John 10:30; Matthew 28:19; John 14:16-17; 1 John 5:7-8 and Colossians 2:9)

Chapter 13: If God is Good

What would this world look like if we didn't have evil? Will evil ever cease? (Genesis 2:10-14; Ezekiel 28:13; Genesis 3:15-19; Romans 5:12; John 16:33; Ephesians 6:12; James 1:13; James 4:4; Isaiah 5:20; Genesis 6:5 and 1 John: 2:16)

NOTES

NOTES

NOTES

NOTES

NOTES